all-new Low-Carb COOKBOOK

CHEDDARY SAUSAGE FRITTATA

MAKES 4 SERVINGS

4 eggs
¼ cup milk
1 package (12 ounces) bulk breakfast pork sausage
1 poblano pepper,* seeded and chopped
1 cup (4 ounces) shredded Cheddar cheese

Preheat broiler. Mix eggs and milk in bowl; set aside. Heat 12-inch ovenproof nonstick skillet over medium-high heat until hot. (If skillet is not ovenproof, wrap handle in heavy-duty foil.) Add sausage; cook and stir 4 minutes or until no longer pink. Drain sausage on paper towels; set aside. Add poblano to skillet; cook and stir 2 minutes or until crisp-tender. Return sausage to skillet with egg mixture; stir. Cover; cook over medium-low heat 10 minutes or until eggs are almost set. Sprinkle with cheese; broil 2 minutes or until cheese is melted. Cut into 4 wedges.

NUTRIENTS PER SERVING			
Calories	**498**	Cholesterol	**292mg**
Total fat	**39g**	Sodium	**673mg**
Protein	**24g**	Fiber	**<1g**
Carbohydrate	**5g**		

DEEP SOUTH HAM AND REDEYE GRAVY

MAKES 4 SERVINGS

1 tablespoon butter
1 ham steak (about 1⅓ pounds)
1 cup strong coffee
¾ teaspoon sugar
¼ teaspoon hot pepper sauce

Heat skillet over medium-high heat until hot. Add butter; tilt skillet to coat bottom. Add ham; cook 3 minutes. Turn; cook 2 minutes or until lightly browned. Remove ham to serving platter; keep warm. Add remaining ingredients to same skillet. Bring to a boil over high heat; boil 2 to 3 minutes or until reduced to ¼ cup, scraping up any brown bits. Serve gravy over ham.

NUTRIENTS PER SERVING			
Calories	**215**	Cholesterol	**76mg**
Total fat	**9g**	Sodium	**2mg**
Protein	**30g**	Fiber	**0g**
Carbohydrate	**1g**		

CHEDDARY SAUSAGE FRITTATA

NO–KNEAD SANDWICH BREAD

MAKES 30 (^{1}/$_4$-INCH-SLICE) SERVINGS

2 packages (2¼ teaspoons) active dry yeast
¾ cup warm water (110° to 115°F)
3 tablespoons canola oil
1 cup all-purpose flour
⅔ cup uncooked old-fashioned oats
¼ cup soy flour*
¼ cup wheat gluten*
¼ cup sesame seeds*
2 teaspoons sugar substitute
1 teaspoon salt

*Soy flour, wheat gluten and sesame seeds are available in the natural foods sections of many supermarkets and at health food stores.

1. Stir yeast into water in small bowl; let stand 5 minutes. Add oil.

2. Combine all-purpose flour, oats, soy flour, gluten, sesame seeds, sugar substitute and salt in food processor fitted with plastic dough blade. Using on/off pulsing action, process until blended.

3. With processor running, slowly pour yeast mixture through feed tube; then using on/off pulsing action, process until dough comes together and forms a mass. Unlock processor lid, but do not remove; let dough rise 1 hour or until doubled in bulk.

4. Spray 8×4×2-inch loaf pan with nonstick cooking spray. Using on/off pulsing action, process briefly until dough comes together and forms a ball. Turn dough onto floured work surface. Shape into disc. (Dough will be slightly sticky.) Roll dough on floured surface into 12×8-inch rectangle. Roll up from short side; fold under ends and place in prepared pan. Cover with towel; let rise in warm place 45 minutes or until doubled in bulk.

5. Preheat oven to 375°F. Bake 35 minutes or until bread is golden brown and sounds hollow when tapped. Remove from pan and cool completely on wire rack. Cut into ¼-inch slices with serrated knife.

NUTRIENTS PER SERVING			
Calories	**51**	Cholesterol	**0mg**
Total fat	**2g**	Sodium	**79mg**
Protein	**2g**	Fiber	**1g**
Carbohydrate	**6g**		

TWO–MINUTE TUNA SALAD SANDWICH

MAKES 3 SERVINGS

1 6-ounce can water-packed solid albacore tuna, drained and flaked
½ cup sliced celery
2 tablespoons plus 1½ teaspoons mayonnaise or reduced-fat mayonnaise (not nonfat)
1 tablespoon drained capers
½ teaspoon onion powder
6 (¼-inch-thick) slices No-Knead Sandwich Bread (page 6)
Lettuce leaves

1. Combine all ingredients except bread and lettuce in small bowl; mix well.

2. Spread ⅓ tuna mixture on each of 3 bread slices. Top with lettuce leaves and remaining bread slices.

NUTRIENTS PER SERVING			
Calories	**261**	Cholesterol	**31mg**
Total fat	**15g**	Sodium	**560mg**
Protein	**18g**	Fiber	**2g**
Carbohydrate	**12g**		

NO–KNEAD SANDWICH BREAD

CIOPPINO

MAKES 4 SERVINGS

1 teaspoon olive oil
1 large onion, chopped
1 cup sliced celery, with celery tops
1 clove garlic, minced
4 cups water
1 fish-flavored bouillon cube
1 tablespoon salt-free Italian herb seasoning
¼ pound cod or other boneless mild-flavored fish fillets
1 large tomato, chopped
1 can (10 ounces) baby clams, rinsed and drained (optional)
¼ pound uncooked small shrimp, peeled and deveined
¼ pound uncooked bay scallops
¼ cup flaked crabmeat or crabmeat blend
2 tablespoons fresh lemon juice

1. Heat olive oil in large saucepan over medium heat until hot. Add onion, celery and garlic. Cook and stir 5 minutes or until onion is soft. Add water, bouillon cube and Italian seasoning. Cover and bring to a boil over high heat.

2. Cut fish into ½-inch pieces. Add cod and tomato to saucepan. Reduce heat to medium-low; simmer about 5 minutes or until fish is opaque. Add clams, if desired, shrimp, scallops, crabmeat and lemon juice; simmer about 5 minutes or until shrimp and scallops are opaque.

Prep and Cook Time: 30 minutes

NUTRIENTS PER SERVING			
Calories	**122**	Cholesterol	**75mg**
Total fat	**2g**	Sodium	**412mg**
Protein	**18g**	Fiber	**2g**
Carbohydrate	**8g**		

CIOPPINO

SZECHWAN SEAFOOD STIR–FRY

MAKES 4 SERVINGS

1 package (10 ounces) fresh spinach leaves
4 teaspoons dark sesame oil, divided
4 cloves garlic, minced and divided
¼ cup reduced-sodium soy sauce
1 tablespoon cornstarch
1 tablespoon dry sherry or sake
1 medium red bell pepper, cut into thin, 1-inch-long strips
1½ teaspoons minced fresh or bottled ginger root
¾ pound peeled deveined large uncooked shrimp, thawed if frozen
½ pound fresh bay scallops
2 teaspoons sesame seeds, toasted

1. Rinse spinach in cold water; drain. Heat 2 teaspoons sesame oil in large saucepan over medium heat. Add 2 cloves garlic; stir-fry 1 minute. Add spinach; cover and steam 4 to 5 minutes or until spinach is wilted, turning with tongs after 3 minutes. Remove from heat; cover.

2. Meanwhile, combine soy sauce, cornstarch and sherry in small bowl; stir until smooth. Set aside. Heat remaining 2 teaspoons sesame oil in large nonstick skillet over medium-high heat. Add bell pepper; stir-fry 2 minutes. Add remaining 2 cloves garlic and ginger; stir-fry 1 minute. Add shrimp; stir-fry 2 minutes. Add scallops; stir-fry 1 minute or until shrimp and scallops are opaque. Add soy sauce mixture; stir-fry 1 minute or until sauce thickens.

3. Stir spinach mixture; divide evenly among 4 individual plates. Top with seafood mixture and sesame seeds.

Tip: Substitute one large head bok choy, thinly sliced, for spinach. Increase steaming time to 8 minutes or until bok choy is tender.

NUTRIENTS PER SERVING			
Calories	**249**	Cholesterol	**147mg**
Total fat	**9g**	Sodium	**960mg**
Protein	**31g**	Fiber	**7g**
Carbohydrate	**10g**		

SZECHWAN SEAFOOD STIR-FRY

SPINACH, CHEESE AND PROSCIUTTO–STUFFED CHICKEN BREASTS

MAKES 4 SERVINGS

4 boneless skinless chicken breasts (about 4 ounces each)
   Salt and black pepper
4 slices (½ ounce each) prosciutto*
4 slices (½ ounce each) smoked provolone
1 cup spinach leaves, chopped
4 tablespoons all-purpose flour, divided
1 tablespoon olive oil
1 tablespoon butter
1 cup chicken broth
1 tablespoon heavy cream

*Prosciutto, an Italian ham, is seasoned, cured and air-dried, not smoked. Look for imported or domestic prosciutto in delis and Italian food markets.

1. Preheat oven to 350°F.

2. To form pocket, cut each chicken breast horizontally almost to opposite edge. Fold back top half of breast; sprinkle lightly with salt and pepper. Place 1 slice prosciutto, 1 slice provolone and ¼ cup spinach on each chicken breast. Fold top half of breasts over filling.

3. Spread 3 tablespoons flour on plate. Holding chicken breast closed, coat in flour; shake off excess. Lightly sprinkle chicken with salt and pepper.

4. Heat oil and butter in large skillet over medium heat. Place chicken in skillet; cook about 4 minutes on each side or until browned. Transfer chicken to shallow baking dish. Bake in oven 10 minutes or until chicken is no longer pink and juices run clear.

5. Meanwhile, whisk chicken broth and cream into remaining 1 tablespoon flour in small bowl. Pour chicken broth mixture into same skillet; heat over medium heat, stirring constantly, until sauce thickens, about 3 minutes. Spoon sauce onto serving plates; top with chicken breasts.

Tip: Swiss, Gruyére or mozzarella cheese can be substituted for smoked provolone. Thinly sliced deli ham can be substituted for prosciutto.

NUTRIENTS PER SERVING			
Calories	**371**	Cholesterol	**105mg**
Total fat	**23g**	Sodium	**854mg**
Protein	**33g**	Fiber	**<1g**
Carbohydrate	**7g**		

SPINACH, CHEESE AND PROSCIUTTO–STUFFED CHICKEN BREAST

PORK CURRY OVER CAULIFLOWER COUSCOUS

MAKES 6 SERVINGS

3 tablespoons olive oil, divided
2 tablespoons mild curry powder
2 teaspoons minced garlic
1½ pounds pork (boneless shoulder, loin or chops), cut into 1-inch cubes
1 red or green bell pepper, seeded and diced
1 tablespoon cider vinegar
½ teaspoon salt
2 cups water
1 large head cauliflower

1. Heat 2 tablespoons oil in large saucepan over medium heat. Add curry powder and garlic; cook and stir 1 to 2 minutes or until garlic is golden.

2. Add pork; stir to coat completely with curry and garlic. Cook and stir 5 to 7 minutes or until pork cubes are barely pink in center. Add bell pepper and vinegar; cook and stir 3 minutes or until bell pepper is soft. Sprinkle with salt.

3. Add water; bring to a boil. Reduce heat and simmer 30 to 45 minutes, stirring occasionally, until liquid is reduced and pork is tender, adding additional water as needed.

4. Meanwhile, trim and core cauliflower; cut into equal pieces. Place in food processor fitted with metal blade. Process using on/off pulsing action until cauliflower is in small uniform pieces about the size of cooked couscous. *Do not purée.*

5. Heat remaining 1 tablespoon oil over medium heat in 12-inch nonstick skillet. Add cauliflower; cook and stir 5 minutes or until crisp-tender. *Do not overcook.* Serve pork curry over cauliflower.

NUTRIENTS PER SERVING			
Calories	**267**	Cholesterol	**69mg**
Total fat	**15g**	Sodium	**308mg**
Protein	**28g**	Fiber	**5g**
Carbohydrate	**7g**		

PORK CURRY OVER CAULIFLOWER COUSCOUS

BLUE CHEESE–STUFFED SIRLOIN PATTIES

MAKES 4 SERVINGS

1½ **pounds ground beef sirloin**
½ **cup (2 ounces) shredded sharp Cheddar cheese**
¼ **cup crumbled blue cheese**
¼ **cup finely chopped fresh parsley**
2 **teaspoons Dijon mustard**
1 **teaspoon Worcestershire sauce**
1 **clove garlic, minced**
¼ **teaspoon salt**
2 **teaspoons olive oil**
1 **medium red bell pepper, cut into thin strips**

1. Shape beef into 8 patties, about 4 inches in diameter and ¼ inch thick.

2. Combine cheeses, parsley, mustard, Worcestershire sauce, garlic and salt in small bowl; toss gently to blend.

3. Mound ¼ of cheese mixture on each of 4 patties (about 3 tablespoons per patty). Top with remaining 4 patties; pinch edges of patties to seal completely. Set aside.

4. Heat oil in 12-inch nonstick skillet over medium-high heat until hot. Add pepper strips; cook and stir until edges begin to brown. Sprinkle with salt. Remove from skillet and keep warm.

5. Add beef patties to same skillet; cook over medium-high heat 5 minutes. Turn patties; top with peppers. Cook 4 minutes or until patties are no longer pink (160°F).

NUTRIENTS PER SERVING			
Calories	**463**	Cholesterol	**131mg**
Total fat	**32g**	Sodium	**548mg**
Protein	**38g**	Fiber	**1g**
Carbohydrate	**3g**		

BLUE CHEESE–STUFFED SIRLOIN PATTY

JALAPEÑO WILD RICE CAKES

MAKES 8 SERVINGS

¾ cup water
⅓ cup uncooked wild rice
½ teaspoon salt, divided
1 tablespoon all-purpose flour
½ teaspoon baking powder
1 egg
1 jalapeño pepper,* finely chopped
2 tablespoons minced onion
1 tablespoon freshly grated ginger *or* 2 teaspoons ground ginger
2 tablespoons vegetable or olive oil

Jalapeño peppers can sting and irritate the skin; wear rubber gloves when handling peppers and do not touch eyes. Wash hands after handling.

1. Combine water, rice and ¼ teaspoon salt in medium saucepan. Bring to a boil. Reduce heat; cover and simmer 40 to 45 minutes or until rice is tender. Drain rice, if necessary; place in medium bowl. Add flour, baking powder and remaining ¼ teaspoon salt; mix until blended.

2. Whisk egg, jalapeño pepper, onion and ginger together in small bowl. Pour egg mixture over rice; mix until well blended.

3. Heat oil in large nonstick skillet over medium heat. Spoon 2 tablespoons rice mixture into pan and shape into cake. Cook, 4 cakes at a time, 3 minutes on each side or until golden brown. Transfer to paper towels. Serve immediately or refrigerate rice cakes for up to 24 hours.

Tip: To reheat cold rice cakes, preheat oven to 400°F. Place rice cakes in single layer on baking sheet; heat 5 minutes.

NUTRIENTS PER SERVING			
Calories	63	Cholesterol	27mg
Total fat	4g	Sodium	330mg
Protein	2g	Fiber	<1g
Carbohydrate	5g		

JALAPEÑO WILD RICE CAKES

ASPARAGUS WITH SESAME–GINGER SAUCE

MAKES 7 SERVINGS

1 tablespoon SPLENDA® Granular
1 tablespoon water
1 tablespoon peanut oil
1 tablespoon rice vinegar
1 tablespoon soy sauce
1 tablespoon tahini* (puréed sesame seeds)
1 teaspoon chopped fresh ginger
½ teaspoon chopped garlic
   Pinch crushed red pepper
48 medium asparagus spears, trimmed and peeled

*Look for tahini in the ethnic foods section of your supermarket.

1. In a food processor, combine all ingredients except asparagus and mix until thoroughly blended. Set aside.

2. Fill large skillet half-full of water; cover and bring to a boil. Add asparagus and simmer just until crisp-tender, approximately 4 to 5 minutes. Drain well. (Do not rinse.)

3. Transfer to serving platter. Pour sauce over hot asparagus. Serve warm or at room temperature.

Prep Time: 10 minutes
Cook Time: 5 minutes

NUTRIENTS PER SERVING			
Calories	59	Cholesterol	0mg
Total fat	3g	Sodium	183mg
Protein	3g	Fiber	2g
Carbohydrate	6g		

ASPARAGUS WITH SESAME–GINGER SAUCE

CHICKEN SALAD

MAKES 4 SERVINGS

¼ cup *each* mayonnaise and sour cream
1 tablespoon lemon juice
1 teaspoon *each* sugar, grated lemon peel and Dijon mustard
½ teaspoon salt
⅛ to ¼ teaspoon white pepper
2 cups diced cooked chicken
1 cup sliced celery
¼ cup sliced green onions
Lettuce leaves

Mix mayonnaise, sour cream, lemon juice, sugar, lemon peel, mustard, salt and pepper. Add chicken, celery and onions; stir. Cover; chill at least 1 hour. Serve salad on lettuce-lined plates.

NUTRIENTS PER SERVING			
Calories	310	Cholesterol	69mg
Total fat	23g	Sodium	442mg
Protein	22g	Fiber	1g
Carbohydrate	4g		

RASPBERRY MANGO SALAD

MAKES 4 SERVINGS

2 cups arugula
1 cup torn Bibb or Boston lettuce
½ cup watercress, stems removed
1 cup diced mango
¾ cup fresh raspberries
¼ cup (1½ ounces) crumbled blue cheese
1 tablespoon *each* olive oil, water and raspberry vinegar
⅛ teaspoon *each* salt and black pepper

Mix arugula, lettuce, watercress, mango, raspberries and cheese in medium bowl. Shake remaining ingredients in small jar. Pour dressing over salad; toss to coat. Serve immediately.

NUTRIENTS PER SERVING			
Calories	98	Cholesterol	8mg
Total fat	8g	Sodium	227mg
Protein	3g	Fiber	2g
Carbohydrate	4g		

RASPBERRY MANGO SALAD

THAI BROCCOLI SALAD

MAKES 4 SERVINGS

¼ cup creamy or chunky peanut butter
2 tablespoons EQUAL® SPOONFUL*
1½ tablespoons hot water
1 tablespoon lime juice
1 tablespoon light soy sauce
1½ teaspoons dark sesame oil
¼ teaspoon red pepper flakes
2 tablespoons vegetable oil
3 cups fresh broccoli florets
½ cup chopped red bell pepper
¼ cup sliced green onions
1 clove garlic, crushed

*May substitute 3 packets Equal® sweetener.

• Combine peanut butter, Equal®, hot water, lime juice, soy sauce, sesame oil and red pepper flakes until well blended; set aside.

• Heat vegetable oil in large skillet over medium-high heat. Add broccoli, red pepper, green onions and garlic. Stir-fry 3 to 4 minutes until vegetables are tender-crisp. Remove from heat and stir in peanut butter mixture.

• Serve warm or at room temperature.

NUTRIENTS PER SERVING			
Calories	199	Cholesterol	0mg
Total fat	17g	Sodium	342mg
Protein	6g	Fiber	4g
Carbohydrate	9g		

THAI BROCCOLI SALAD

HAM AND CHEESE "SUSHI" ROLLS

MAKES 8 SERVINGS

4 thin slices deli ham (about 4×4 inches)
1 package (8 ounces) cream cheese, softened
1 seedless cucumber, quartered lengthwise and cut into 4-inch lengths
4 thin slices (about 4×4 inches) American or Cheddar cheese, at room temperature
1 red bell pepper, cut into thin 4-inch long strips

Pat 1 ham slice with paper towel to remove excess moisture. Spread 2 tablespoons cream cheese to edges of ham slice. Pat 1 cucumber quarter with paper towel to remove excess moisture; place at edge of ham slice. Roll tightly, pressing to seal. Wrap in plastic wrap; refrigerate. Repeat with remaining 3 ham slices. Spread 2 tablespoons cream cheese to edges of 1 cheese slice. Place 2 strips red pepper even with edge of cheese slice. Roll tightly, pressing to seal. Wrap in plastic wrap; refrigerate. Repeat with remaining 3 cheese slices. Remove plastic wrap from ham and cheese rolls. Cut each roll into 8 (½-inch-wide) pieces.

NUTRIENTS PER SERVING			
Calories	**145**	Cholesterol	**40mg**
Total fat	**13g**	Sodium	**263mg**
Protein	**5g**	Fiber	**<1g**
Carbohydrate	**3g**		

WILD WEDGES

MAKES 4 SERVINGS

2 (8-inch) fat-free flour tortillas
⅓ cup shredded reduced-fat Cheddar cheese
⅓ cup chopped cooked chicken or turkey
1 green onion, thinly sliced (about ¼ cup)
2 tablespoons mild, thick and chunky salsa

Heat large nonstick skillet over medium heat until hot. Spray one side of one flour tortilla with nonstick cooking spray; place sprayed side down in skillet. Top with cheese, chicken, green onion and salsa. Place remaining tortilla over mixture; spray with cooking spray. Cook 2 to 3 minutes per side or until golden brown and cheese is melted. Cut into 8 triangles.

NUTRIENTS PER SERVING			
Calories	**82**	Cholesterol	**13mg**
Total fat	**2g**	Sodium	**224mg**
Protein	**7g**	Fiber	**3g**
Carbohydrate	**8g**		

HAM AND CHEESE "SUSHI" ROLLS

CHOCOLATE–ALMOND MERINGUE PUFFS

MAKES 15 SERVINGS

    2 tablespoons granulated sugar
    3 packages sugar substitute
1½ teaspoons unsweetened cocoa powder
    2 egg whites, room temperature
 ½ teaspoon vanilla
 ¼ teaspoon cream of tartar
 ¼ teaspoon almond extract
 ⅛ teaspoon salt
1½ ounces sliced almonds
    3 tablespoons sugar-free seedless raspberry fruit spread

1. Preheat oven to 275°F. Combine granulated sugar, sugar substitute and cocoa powder in small bowl; set aside.

2. Beat egg whites in small bowl with electric mixer at high speed until foamy. Add vanilla, cream of tartar, almond extract and salt; beat until soft peaks form. Add sugar mixture, 1 tablespoon at a time, beating until stiff peaks form.

3. Line baking sheet with foil. Spoon 15 equal mounds of egg white mixture onto foil. Sprinkle with almonds.

4. Bake 1 hour. Turn oven off but do not open oven door. Leave puffs in oven 2 hours longer or until completely dry. Remove from oven; cool completely.

5. Stir fruit spread; spoon about ½ teaspoon onto each meringue just before serving.

Tip: Puffs are best if eaten the same day they're made. If necessary, store in airtight container, adding fruit topping just before serving.

NUTRIENTS PER SERVING			
Calories	**34**	Cholesterol	**0mg**
Total fat	**1g**	Sodium	**27mg**
Protein	**1g**	Fiber	**<1g**
Carbohydrate	**4g**		

CHOCOLATE-ALMOND MERINGUE PUFFS

CHOCOLATE CHEESECAKE
MAKES 10 SERVINGS

2 packages (8 ounces each) cream cheese, softened
2 eggs
⅓ cup plus 2 teaspoons granular sugar substitute,* divided
2 tablespoons honey
3 teaspoons vanilla, divided
2 level tablespoons unsweetened cocoa
1 cup heavy whipping cream

*Choose a sugar substitute that measures like sugar, such as Splenda® or Equal® Spoonful.

1. Preheat oven to 350°F. Spray 8-inch round cake pan with nonstick cooking spray. Cut 8-inch parchment paper or wax paper circle to fit bottom of pan. Place paper in pan; spray lightly with cooking spray.

2. Combine cream cheese, eggs, ⅓ cup sugar substitute, honey and 2 teaspoons vanilla in large bowl; beat with electric mixer at medium speed 2 to 3 minutes just until well blended. With mixer at low speed, beat in cocoa until well blended. *Do not overbeat.*

3. Pour batter into prepared pan. Bake 35 to 40 minutes or until center is set. Cool 10 minutes on wire rack; run thin spatula around edge of cheesecake to loosen. Cool completely.

4. Invert cheesecake onto plate. Remove parchment paper. Place serving plate over cake; invert cake top side up. Cover loosely with plastic wrap. Refrigerate at least 4 hours or overnight.

5. Beat cream, remaining 2 teaspoons sugar substitute and 1 teaspoon vanilla in small deep bowl with electric mixer at high speed until stiff peaks form. Serve with cheesecake.

NUTRIENTS PER SERVING			
Calories	296	Cholesterol	125mg
Total fat	27g	Sodium	158mg
Protein	6g	Fiber	<1g
Carbohydrate	7g		